Figurative Language Quick Starts

Author: Jane Heitman
Editor: Mary Dieterich
Proofreaders: Margaret Brown and April Albert

COPYRIGHT © 2019 Mark Twain Media, Inc.

ISBN 978-1-62223-770-8

Printing No. CD-405036

Mark Twain Media, Inc., Publishers
Distributed by Carson-Dellosa Publishing LLC

Visit www.carsondellosa.com

Table of Contents

Introduction to the Teacher

Use these Quick Start activities to introduce, reinforce, and review figurative language concepts. They can help students isolate and identify figurative language techniques in literature and give them practice for their own writing. Students may use the Quick Starts to begin a new piece of writing, to edit a piece already written, or to generate ideas later. They will practice using contextual clues to complete some of the activities.

Activities include multiple choice, fill-in-the-blank, concept application, and creative responses. Some activities may require the teacher's help in finding library or Internet resources where students can find answers. The activities explain and illustrate each of the 11 types of figurative language included and offer students an opportunity to play with language.

The Quick Starts can be used in any order, at any time, and require simple classroom materials and access to a library. Paper, pencil or pen, and a photocopy of the reproducible are all students need to get started. To assess their work, you may use student self-check, extra credit, or a point system.

To use the pages, reproduce them and cut along the lines to provide students with mini-lessons. You can also reproduce pages and distribute them whole for students to keep in a folder or binder. Pages may also be kept in a learning center for students to work on as enrichment activities.

Your students can get a quick start with figurative language as they learn about, explore, and enjoy the richness of the English language.

Imagery

IMAGERY 1

Imagery (IM-uj-ree) uses words to paint a picture in the reader's mind.

Write a short description of this scene, painting a picture with words.

_____

_____

_____

_____

_____

_____

_____

IMAGERY 2

Imagery describes sights to paint a word picture.

Underline the imagery in this paragraph:

A blue pottery bowl sat on the

kitchen counter. The bowl held

yellow bananas with black-flecked

skin, large red apples, and pale

green pears.

IMAGERY 3

Imagery describes sounds to interest readers.

Write five sound words here.

_____

_____

_____

_____

_____

Imagery

IMAGERY 4

Imagery describes smells to help the reader enter the scene.

Imagine you are at a carnival. Write five things you smell.

_____

_____

_____

_____

_____

IMAGERY 5

Imagery describes tastes to interest readers.

Write five taste words here.

_____

_____

_____

_____

_____

IMAGERY 6

Choose your favorite food. Use imagery to describe the food to someone who has never seen it.

_____

_____

_____

_____

_____

_____

_____

IMAGERY 7

Imagery describes how things feel so readers can imagine the experience.

Draw lines between the words that describe a feeling and the thing they describe.

1. scratchy   a. wool sweater

2. nubby   b. angora fur

3. silky   c. pillow

4. rough   d. carpet

5. soft   e. sandpaper

Imagery

IMAGERY 8

Underline the words in the paragraph below that describe the five senses: sight, sound, smell, taste, and touch.

I opened one eye when my alarm clock buzzed. My room was still dark, but I could smell coffee. When the scent of sizzling bacon hit my nose, my mouth watered and my stomach growled. I knew Mom would cook it until it was crunchy, just the way I like it. My feet met the cold, hard floor as I got out of bed. I threw on my soft, red sweatshirt and jeans and headed for breakfast.

IMAGERY 9

Look at your pen or pencil. Write one word or phrase about it for each of the five senses.

Sight: _____

Sound: _____

Smell: _____

Taste: _____

Touch: _____

IMAGERY 10

How does each of the following feel when you touch it? Write a touch word for each.

sidewalk _____

grass _____

ice cream _____

water _____

tree trunk _____

Imagery

IMAGERY 11

Imagery uses specific words to paint an accurate picture. For example, using *Irish Setter* instead of *dog* tells the reader what kind of dog.

Write a specific word for the general ones below.

cereal _____

flower _____

person _____

shoes _____

music _____

IMAGERY 12

Circle the words that are specific.

ocean   basketball

cottonwood   movie

sport   Lake Erie

aloe vera   house

plant   *Black Panther*

one-bedroom apartment

IMAGERY 13

Fill in each blank with a specific word. A general hint is given.

The (boy) _____

visited the (mountains) _____

_____ with his

(family) _____.

They caught (fish) _____

in the (creek) _____

and cooked them for (a meal)

_____.

IMAGERY 14

On your own paper, describe today's weather. Remember to use imagery and as many of the five senses (sight, sound, smell, taste, touch) as you can.

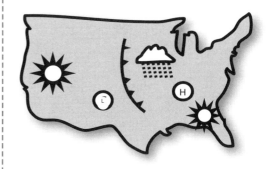

Imagery

IMAGERY 15

Imagery uses details to make something stand out.

Write the unique detail about each mug beneath it.

1.

2.

3.

_____

_____

_____

_____

_____

_____

_____

_____

_____

IMAGERY 16

Circle the words that describe taste.

spicy   hard

blue   sweet

peppery   sour

noisy   bland

blunt   fruity

itchy   cloudy

IMAGERY 17

Circle the words that describe textures (touch).

red   smooth

rough   spicy

hard   lemony

sharp   large

shiny   crusty

Imagery

IMAGERY 18

Onomatopoeia (ON-uh-MAH-tuh-PEE-uh) means "a word that sounds like what it is." Two examples are *buzz* and *zoom*. Think of three more and write them below.

1. _____

2. _____

3. _____

IMAGERY 19

Circle the words that describe sounds.

cry	dirt	splat
fell	brown	yellow
bark	thud	gurgle
tap	clomp	wooden
cheese	clap	swish

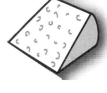

IMAGERY 20

With imagery, write sentences that describe a slice of pizza to someone who cannot see.

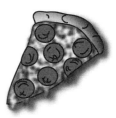

_____

_____

_____

_____

_____

Simile

SIMILE 1

A **simile** (SIM-uh-lee) compares two unlike things using the words *like* or *as.*

Underline the sentences below that are similes.

1.   Love is a rose.

2.   Love is like a rose.

3.   Love is as thorny as a rose.

4.   Love is found in a rose garden.

SIMILE 2

Finish this sentence with a simile.

Going to the dentist is like _____

_____

_____

_____

SIMILE 3

What do these similes mean?

March comes in like a lion and goes out like a lamb.

_____

_____

_____

SIMILE 4

Write your own simile by filling in the blank.

_____

_____

_____

as the wind.

Simile

SIMILE 5

A **simile** (SIM-uh-lee) compares two unlike things using the words *like* or *as*.

What two things are being compared in this sentence?

The girl laughed like a hyena.

_____

_____

SIMILE 6

Draw lines connecting the phrases below so they create appropriate similes.

1. The opera star sang   like sardines.

2. Seven people in the compact   like a three-ring circus.
   car were packed

3. The preschool children were   like a nightingale.
   so wild, the room was

SIMILE 7

Many similes use animal comparisons. Draw lines to
connect the trait to the animal.

1. Sly as   a lamb

2. Quiet as   an owl

3   Gentle as   a fox

4. Wise as   a mouse

Simile

SIMILE 8

Circle the phrase that best completes the sentence.

A sunny day is like:

a snowman.

a song.

a good lunch.

SIMILE 9

Write your own simile by completing the sentence.

A rainy day is like _____

_____

_____.

SIMILE 10

Write your own simile by completing the sentence.

_____

_____

smells like a wet dog.

SIMILE 11

Underline the sentence below that contains a simile.

My dog smells like gym socks.

My dog smells his dinner.

My cat smells my dog.

Simile

SIMILE 12

Imagine you must explain "sky" to someone who has never seen it. Write a short description on these lines. Use similes where you can. Begin with the words, "The sky is like…"

_____

_____

_____

_____

_____

_____

_____

_____

SIMILE 13

1. Write three similes using the word *like.*

   _____

   _____

   _____

2. Write three similes using the word *as.*

   _____

   _____

   _____

SIMILE 14

Complete the following sentence:

The movie was as boring as _____

_____

_____.

Complete the following sentence:

_____

_____

_____

was as thrilling as a roller coaster.

Simile

SIMILE 15

Use at least two of the words below to create an appropriate simile. Write it below.

jeans   happiness   heart
snail   flower   pizza
peace   ring

_____

_____

_____

_____

SIMILE 16

Complete the following sentence.

My pet dinosaur is like _____

_____

_____,

because _____

_____

_____.

SIMILE 17

How is the following simile true? Think of as many ways as you can.

A race car is like an athlete.

_____

_____

_____

_____

_____

_____

SIMILE 18

Underline the simile below.

A rainbow is a prism.

A rainbow is a beautiful display in the sky.

A rainbow is like a box of crayons.

The colors of white light are visible in a rainbow.

Metaphor

METAPHOR 1

A **metaphor** (MET-uh-for) compares two unlike things directly, without using *like* or *as.*

Underline the sentence below that is a metaphor.

Love is a rose.

Love is like a rose.

Love is an emotion.

METAPHOR 2

What does the following metaphor mean? Put a check next to the correct answer.

My grandfather is a turtle.

_____ My grandfather has a hard shell.

_____ My grandfather is green.

_____ My grandfather is slow.

METAPHOR 3

Carl Sandburg wrote, "The fog comes on little cat feet." In what ways is fog like a cat? Write your answer below. Ask your teacher to help you find the rest of Sandburg's poem, "Fog."

_____

_____

_____

_____

_____

_____

Metaphor

METAPHOR 4

Shakespeare wrote, "Shall I compare thee to a summer's day?" (Sonnet 18)

Write a metaphor below that compares someone to a summer day.

_____

_____

_____

_____

METAPHOR 5

What two things are being compared, and what does the comparison mean? Write your answer below.

I can't go to the movie tonight. I'm under an avalanche of homework.

_____

_____

_____

_____

METAPHOR 6

Write your own metaphor by completing the sentence below. Then write the ways in which your metaphor is true.

Happiness is _____

_____

This is true because _____

_____

_____

METAPHOR 7

What is being compared in the metaphor below? What does it mean? Write your answer below.

Has your train of thought jumped its track?

_____

is compared to _____.

This means _____

_____.

Metaphor

METAPHOR 8

Charles Schulz, the creator of the *Peanuts* comic strip, wrote a book called *Happiness is a Warm Puppy*. In what ways is that title true? Write your answer below.

_____

_____

_____

_____

_____

METAPHOR 9

Ann's mom called Ann the "Birthday Queen."

Is Ann royalty?

Circle one: Yes   No

What does Ann's mom mean?

_____

_____

_____

_____

METAPHOR 10

Write a metaphor comparing a weather condition to an animal.

_____

_____

In what ways is this true?

_____

_____

_____

_____

Metaphor

METAPHOR 11

Write a metaphor describing someone who is angry.

_____

_____

_____

This is true because _____

_____

_____.

METAPHOR 12

Steven snaked his way through the crowd.

What is being compared?

_____

_____

On your own paper, draw Steven's path.

METAPHOR 13

The sentences below mean almost the same thing. The difference is in the effect each sentence has on the reader. On your own paper, describe the differences. (Hint: how do you react to each sentence's comparison?)

Love is a rose.

Love is like a rose.

METAPHOR 14

"My classroom is an oven" means (check the correct choice):

_____ My classroom contains ovens.

_____ My classroom is hot.

_____ My classroom is for baking.

Metaphor

METAPHOR 15

Fill in the blank with your own metaphor.

The school cafeteria is

_____

_____.

In what ways is this true?

_____

_____

_____

METAPHOR 16

"The star was a publicity magnet."

In what ways is this metaphor true?

_____

_____

_____

_____

METAPHOR 17

Poetry often contains metaphors to help readers see things in a new way. Use one of the metaphors you have written or write a new one. Then create a poem with that metaphor.

_____

_____

_____

_____

_____

_____

_____

_____

Metaphor

METAPHOR 18

Look for three metaphors today. They could be anywhere—newspapers, textbooks, library books, magazines, websites, social media posts—anywhere there's print! Write them below and tell where you found them:

1. _____

2. _____

3. _____

METAPHOR 19

"The teacher was iron about following rules" means (check the correct choice):

_____   The teacher ironed clothes while students followed the rules.

_____   The teacher would not bend or break the rules.

_____   The teacher was not good at following rules.

METAPHOR 20

Describe your day metaphorically.

Today is _____

_____.

This is true because _____

_____.

Adage

ADAGE 1

An **adage** (ADD-uj) is an old, wise saying containing universal truth. Many adages are also metaphors.

"Let sleeping dogs lie" is not really about dogs. What does the adage mean?

_____

_____

_____

ADAGE 2

"Truth is stranger than fiction" is an adage. Find a news story that proves the truth of the adage. Write the headline here, and tell where you found it.

_____

_____

_____

_____

_____

_____

ADAGE 3

Some adages can be modernized.

"A watched pot never boils," is an old adage.

Write a modern version by completing the following sentence:

A listened-for

cell phone never

_____.

ADAGE 4

Imagine you are working on a class project with a group. How might this adage apply?

"Too many cooks spoil the broth."

_____

_____

_____

_____

_____

_____

Adage

ADAGE 5

"Don't bite the hand that feeds you."

Check the sentence below that most closely shows the meaning of the adage.

_____ Don't bite your mother.

_____ Be good to those who provide for you.

_____ Be careful when you eat.

ADAGE 6

"Nothing ventured, nothing gained" is closest in meaning to which other adage listed below? Check the best answer.

_____ Use it or lose it.

_____ No pain, no gain.

_____ Where there's a will, there's a way.

DON'T MISS OUT!
$ $ INVESTMENT $
OPPORTUNITY! $ $
INFO MEETING 7 PM TONIGHT!

ADAGE 7

How can this adage be true? "Whether you think you can or you think you can't, you're right."

_____

_____

_____

_____

Adage

ADAGE 8

"Fools and their money are soon parted." On your own paper, write about a time you were sorry you spent money on something that turned out to be foolish.

ADAGE 9

"Two heads are better than one" is an adage.

Create a new saying by completing the sentence below.

Two heads are better than one,

unless _____

_____

_____

_____

ADAGE 10

1. What does the adage "A stitch in time saves nine" mean?

   _____

   _____

   _____

2. If "the early bird gets the worm," what does the late bird get?

   _____

   _____

   _____

ADAGE 11

1. "Silence is golden" is a famous adage. Finish the sentence below using a similar metaphor.

   Noise is _____

   _____

2. Rewrite the adage "If at first you don't succeed, try, try again" by completing the sentence below.

   If at first you don't succeed,

   _____

   _____

Adage

ADAGE 12

These two adages have the opposite meaning. On your own paper, write which one you think is true and why.

"Absence makes the heart grow fonder."

"Out of sight, out of mind."

ADAGE 13

"Early to bed, early to rise, makes a man healthy, wealthy, and wise." Write your own version of this adage:

Early to bed, early to rise, makes a

person _____

_____

_____

_____

_____

ADAGE 14

"All work and no play makes Jack a dull boy" emphasizes the importance of (check the best answer):

_____ work.

_____ brains.

_____ play.

ADAGE 15

"I can't tell you. I have to show you." This best tells the meaning of which adage? Check the correct one below.

_____ All's fair in love and war.

_____ Beauty is in the eye of the beholder.

_____ A picture is worth a thousand words.

Adage

ADAGE 16

On your own paper, draw a cartoon that shows the meaning of the following adage. Use the space below to sketch your ideas.

"One person's junk is another person's treasure."

ADAGE 17

"Ignorance is bliss."

In what ways is this adage true? In what ways is it false? Do you think it is more true or false? Answer the questions in paragraph form on your own paper.

ADAGE 18

"The grass is always greener on the other side of the fence" is closest in meaning to which of the following? Check the correct one.

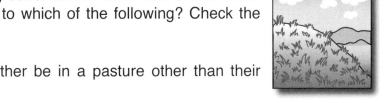

_____ Cows would rather be in a pasture other than their own.

_____ The neighbors take better care of their lawn than you do.

_____ People always think someone else is better off than they are.

Idiom

IDIOM 1

An **idiom** (ID-ee-um) is a saying that does not make literal, logical, or grammatical sense. However, people within the same culture understand the meaning.

What does the idiom "What's the buzz?" mean? Check the correct choice.

_____ Where are the bees?

_____ What's the news?

_____ What time does the end-of-school bell ring?

IDIOM 2

"It's raining cats and dogs" is a common idiom.

On your own paper, draw one picture showing the literal meaning of the saying and one picture showing the actual meaning of the saying.

IDIOM 3

What does "I'm going to hit the hay" mean? Check the correct choice.

_____ I'm going to practice boxing.

_____ I'm going to clean out the barn.

_____ I'm going to bed.

Idiom

IDIOM 4

Before she gave her speech in class, Tanya had butterflies in her stomach. This sentence means (check the best answer):

_____ Tanya had eaten a caterpillar.

_____ Tanya was so nervous that her stomach felt fluttery.

_____ Tanya had a serious disease.

IDIOM 5

Which of the following idioms means "to work late into the night"? Check the best choice.

_____ burn the candle at both ends

_____ burn the midnight oil

_____ burn your bridges

IDIOM 6

Which idiom below has a similar meaning to "Don't let the cat out of the bag"? Check the correct choice.

_____ Mum's the word.

_____ Don't beat around the bush.

_____ Don't go off the deep end.

IDIOM 7

When you have accomplished something great, you might want to (check the best answer):

_____ fly off the handle.

_____ go haywire.

_____ blow your own horn.

Idiom

IDIOM 8

Rewrite the following sentence in standard English. The idioms are in italics.

I'm *all thumbs* at making this craft, but I'll have *to bite the bullet* and do it before it becomes *an albatross around my neck*.

_____

_____

_____

_____

IDIOM 9

Check all the idioms below that mean "grumpy."

____ cold turkey   ____ got up on the wrong side of the bed

____ faced the music   ____ has a bee in her bonnet

____ has his dander up   ____ knows the ropes

IDIOM 10

If someone says, "I'm going whole hog to get your goat," what would you say? Write your answer here.

_____

_____

_____

_____

Idiom

IDIOM 11

Circle the number of the choice that means "I'll do everything I can to help you get the job."

1. I'll go back to the drawing board and call a spade a spade.

2. I'll pull strings and cut the red tape for you.

3. I'll butter up the boss and give you a clean bill of health.

IDIOM 12

"We'd better do this by the book" means "We'd better do this..." (check the best answer):

____ in the library.

____ by the rules.

____ at the bookstore.

IDIOM 13

When Susan said, "That's a fine kettle of fish," you knew (check the best answer):

____ she had cooked a fine seafood stew.

____ she had caught many fish that day.

____ she had to handle a messy situation.

IDIOM 14

Write the meaning of the following sentence:

The singer's first CD was a huge success, but critics feared he was a flash in the pan.

_____

_____

_____

_____

Idiom

IDIOM 15

After cooking a big dinner, the messy kitchen needed some elbow grease. Should you add it to your shopping list? Why or why not? Write your answer below.

_____

_____

_____

_____

_____

IDIOM 16

When I went to visit Grandpa, he was taking forty winks. This means (check the best answer):

_____ he was flirting with Grandma.

_____ he was watching TV.

_____ he was taking a nap.

IDIOM 17

1. On your own paper, write a paragraph or create a cartoon that shows correct use of these idioms:

   a. once in a blue moon

   b. put on the dog

   c. pay the piper

2. "It's a dog's life" is an idiom meaning "life is difficult." On your own paper, write whether you think this idiom is true and why or why not.

IDIOM 18

1. If you rule the roost, you (check the best answer):

   _____ have to clean out the chicken coop.

   _____ have to gather eggs.

   _____ are the boss.

2. If someone says, "I've got a bone to pick with you," you should (check the best answer):

   _____ ask what's wrong.

   _____ say, "Thank you."

   _____ eat with the person.

Cliché

CLICHÉ 1

A **cliché** (klee-SHAY) is a saying that's so common it's no longer interesting. Many metaphors, similes, adages, and idioms are clichés.

Finish these clichés:

1. stubborn as a _____

2. as meek as a _____

3. haste makes _____

4. fall head over _____

5. as fit as a _____

CLICHÉ 2

Good writers try to avoid clichés and write something fresh and original.

"Quiet as a mouse" is a cliché. Write a simile that is not a cliché.

quiet as _____

_____

CLICHÉ 3

Some clichés don't make sense. For example, "happy as a clam." How happy IS a clam, anyway? On your own paper, write a short story about a clam seeking happiness. Try to avoid other clichés.

CLICHÉ 4

Here are two clichés with similar meanings: "like a fish out of water" and "like a square peg in a round hole." What do these clichés mean?

_____

_____

_____

_____

Cliché

CLICHÉ 5

If a friend says, "I slept like a log," is that good? Why or why not?

_____

_____

_____

_____

Z Z Z Z Z

CLICHÉ 6

"Slick as a whistle" is a cliché. Write its meaning below.

_____

_____

_____

_____

_____

_____

CLICHÉ 7

"Hard as nails" is a cliché. Which of the following would be more accurate? Check the correct choice.

____ hard as a diamond

____ hard as a helmet

____ hard as a trigonometry problem

CLICHÉ 8

Finish the cliché by checking the correct choice below.

Silly as a:

____ clown.

____ goose.

____ squirrel.

Cliché

CLICHÉ 9

"Cool as a cucumber" is a cliché. Think of 3 original endings and write them below.

Cool as _____.

Cool as _____.

Cool as _____.

CLICHÉ 10

"Smooth as glass" and "smooth as silk" are similar clichés. Which do you think is more accurate and why? Write a more realistic description of something that is smooth.

_____

_____

_____

CLICHÉ 11

"Easy as pie" is a cliché that means a task is simple. Look up the steps for making a pie. (Ask your teacher for help if you need it.) Does this look easy to you? Why or why not?

_____

_____

_____

Cliché

CLICHÉ 12

"Skinny as a rail" means that someone is very thin. From what you can find out about rails, is this description true? Why or why not? (Ask a teacher for help if you need it.)

_____

_____

_____

CLICHÉ 13

Write an original simile that is more accurate than "happy as a clam."

Happy as _____

_____

_____

_____

CLICHÉ 14

"I'll have your order out in a jiffy," the cafe server said. "In a jiffy" is a cliché. What original phrase or standard English could the server have said to mean the same thing?

_____

_____

_____

Cliché

CLICHÉ 15

The coach's face was red as a beet as he shouted at his losing team.

Write an original paragraph below that shows the coach's anger without using clichés.

_____

_____

_____

_____

_____

CLICHÉ 16

"Like greased lightning" is a cliché meaning "really fast."

Look up the speed of light. (Ask your teacher for help if you need it.) How fast is lightning?

_____

_____

_____

CLICHÉ 17

"Good as gold" is a cliché meaning "good-hearted."

Write an original expression below.

Good as _____

_____

_____

Cliché

CLICHÉ 18

Look and listen for clichés. They are everywhere! In the space below, write three clichés you observe, and tell where you heard or saw them.

_____

_____

_____

_____

CLICHÉ 19

"Red as a beet" is a cliché that could show several conditions. List three below.

_____

_____

_____

_____

CLICHÉ 20

"I was scared to death," the crash victim said. Was she? What could she have said instead to be more accurate?

_____

_____

_____

_____

Personification

PERSONIFICATION 1

Personification (pur-SAWN-i-fi-KA-shun) is figurative language that gives human traits to non-human things.

Underline the personification in this sentence:

The sun smiled down on the hikers.

PERSONIFICATION 2

Underline the personification in this sentence:

The cruel mirror showed Cindy's every flaw.

PERSONIFICATION 3

Underline the personification in these sentences:

1. The star I wished on winked at me.

2. The moon looked down on Earth with a smile.

PERSONIFICATION 4

Underline the personification in these sentences:

1. The trout danced in the stream.

2. The brook babbled a soothing lullaby as it ambled across the field.

Personification

PERSONIFICATION 5

Put a check beside the sentence that best shows personification.

_____ The ocean waved.

_____ The ocean waved goodbye.

PERSONIFICATION 6

Write a sentence with personification using these two words:

wind   whistled

_____

_____

_____

_____

_____

_____

PERSONIFICATION 7

Complete the sentence below:

The moon teaches _____

_____

_____

_____

_____

_____

PERSONIFICATION 8

Fill in the blank to personify the acorn in the sentence below.

The acorn _____

of becoming big and mighty.

Personification

PERSONIFICATION 9

Complete the following sentence:

The mountain remembers _____

_____

_____

_____

PERSONIFICATION 10

Think of an object in your room. What might it be hoping for? Personify the object in the sentence below.

_____ hopes

(Object)

_____

_____

_____

PERSONIFICATION 11

Fill in a verb to personify *ruby* in the sentence below.

The blood-red ruby _____

tragic tales.

PERSONIFICATION 12

Write a sentence with personification using these two words:

rock   wept

_____

_____

_____

_____

_____

Personification

PERSONIFICATION 13

Read the sentence and look for the personification.

The old truck coughed and sputtered.

Which two words are things that humans do?

_____ and _____

PERSONIFICATION 14

Fill in the blanks to personify the chair in the sentences below.

1. The desk chair _____ when the

   student dumped a pile of books on it.

2. Its legs _____ as it was shoved

   across the floor.

PERSONIFICATION 15

Put a check beside the sentence that shows personification.

_____ The cactus blooms in the spring.

_____ The cactus brings us blooms
in the spring.

Personification

PERSONIFICATION 16

Use the words below to create at least two sentences with examples of personification.

ocean	wind	stairs	forest	camel
grinned	caressed	protested	loomed	whispered

_____

_____

_____

_____

_____

PERSONIFICATION 17

Underline the examples of personification in the paragraph below.

Jaycee caught the bus to go downtown to the library. As she gripped her seat tightly, the bus darted through traffic like a soccer player avoiding defenders. When it finally deposited her at the library, Jaycee heaved a sigh of relief. She stepped inside and felt the warm welcome the library always offered her. The comforting sights and smells of the familiar books were like old friends greeting her. She couldn't wait to find a new adventure in one of the books displayed like soldiers waiting to be shipped out on a new mission.

Allusion

ALLUSION 1

An **allusion** (uh-LOOZH-un) is a reference to something well known in literature or history.

"I don't like to hang around with Michael. He's such an Eeyore."

Eeyore is an allusion to what stories? _____

What does the sentence say about Michael's outlook on life? _____

_____

ALLUSION 2

The term "Cinderella story" is a clichéd allusion to the fairy tale. Put a check beside the best meaning for that allusion.

_____ A fairy godmother helps someone.

_____ Someone goes to a party and meets royalty.

_____ Someone from a lowly background becomes highly successful.

ALLUSION 3

"Have you been in Mr. McGregor's garden again?" Put a check beside the statement that best describes the allusion from Peter Rabbit.

_____ "Have you been picking carrots?"

_____ "Have you gotten all muddy?"

_____ "Have you been where you were not supposed to go?"

Allusion

ALLUSION 4

"Behave," the babysitter said, "or I'll send my flying monkeys after you!"

"Flying monkeys" is an allusion to what story?

_____

_____

ALLUSION 5

"She barged in like Goldilocks." What does this allusion to the story "Goldilocks and the Three Bears" mean?

_____

_____

_____

_____

_____

ALLUSION 6

"She found those lost gloves so quickly, she must be Nancy Drew!" Put a check beside the statement that best describes the allusion.

_____ She is a magician.

_____ She is a detective.

_____ She is a store clerk.

ALLUSION 7

"He may be 56 years old, but he's a real Peter Pan." Put a check beside the statement that best describes the allusion.

_____ He can fly.

_____ He leads a gang.

_____ He acts like a boy.

Allusion

ALLUSION 8

Put a check beside the word that best completes the sentence.

If someone's hair is like Rapunzel's, it is

____ red.

____ long.

____ curly.

ALLUSION 9

When the twins' mother came home and saw the mess, she said, "I suppose you're going to blame the Cat in the Hat."

Explain the allusion here:

_____

_____

_____

_____

ALLUSION 10

"She is such a Grinch, she won't let us have a class party."

"She won't let us have a class party. She's a Tin Man who needs a trip to Oz."

The main idea of these sentences is similar. Write it here:

_____

_____

_____

_____

ALLUSION 11

When the group was done roasting marshmallows, Jason put out the campfire. "Smokey would be proud," the camp leader said.

Who is Smokey?

_____

_____

_____

_____

Allusion

ALLUSION 12

Choose the best ending for this sentence:

My kitten's name is Curious George because (check the best answer):

_____ he eats bananas.

_____ he came here on a ship.

_____ he gets into everything.

ALLUSION 13

Check the allusion that best completes this sentence:

When Marissa won the beauty pageant, she knew she was no longer

_____ Raggedy Ann.

_____ Sleeping Beauty.

_____ the Ugly Duckling.

ALLUSION 14

Some sayings are allusions from folklore. "Slow and steady wins the race" is from an Aesop fable called "The Tortoise and the Hare."

Find the story and read it. On your own paper, write your own version of the moral. Ask your teacher for help if you need it.

ALLUSION 15

If someone knocking on your door says, "I'll huff, and I'll puff, and I'll blow your house in," that person is quoting the wolf in (check the best answer):

_____ "Little Red Riding Hood."

_____ "Call of the Wild."

_____ "The Three Little Pigs."

Symbolism

SYMBOLISM 1

Symbolism (SIM-bu-liz-um) is figurative language in which a concrete thing is meant to represent an abstract idea or larger concept. For example, one symbol of the United States is the flag.

Write another symbol for the United States:

_____

_____

SYMBOLISM 2

Check which of the following best symbolizes education.

_____ a diploma

_____ a sports team

_____ a book

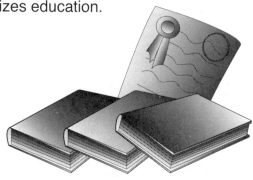

SYMBOLISM 3

Write a statement using *fire* as a symbol for a larger, abstract idea.

_____

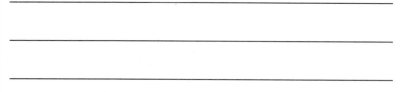

_____

_____

_____

Symbolism

SYMBOLISM 4

School mascots are symbols that show something about their school. Why does your school have the mascot it does? If your school doesn't have a mascot, what would you choose and why? Write your answers on your own paper.

SYMBOLISM 5

Sometimes authors use *spring* to symbolize youth. If that is so, then what would *winter* symbolize?

_____

_____

_____

_____

SYMBOLISM 6

Which of the birds listed below is used to symbolize wisdom? Check the best answer.

_____ loon

_____ owl

_____ eagle

SYMBOLISM 7

Which of the birds listed below is used to symbolize peace? Check the best answer.

_____ swallow

_____ robin

_____ dove

Symbolism

SYMBOLISM 8

Which of the following birds is often used to symbolize war? Check the best answer.

_____ hawk

_____ turkey

_____ vulture

SYMBOLISM 9

Colors are often used as symbols. Their meaning may be different in different cultures.

Check the color that is often used to symbolize life.

_____ pink

_____ brown

_____ green

SYMBOLISM 10

When we say that someone feels blue, blue symbolizes (check the best answer):

_____ fear.

_____ sadness.

_____ anger.

SYMBOLISM 11

In literature, a river is often used to symbolize the journey of life. Check which of the following could also be used.

_____ a jet

_____ a cloud

_____ a road

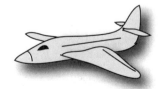

Symbolism

SYMBOLISM 12

Which of the following could a circle symbolize? Check the best answer.

_____ eternity

_____ peace

_____ death

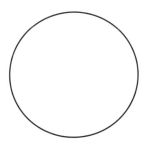

SYMBOLISM 13

What kinds of symbols and colors represent you? Cut a piece of white construction paper, poster board, or card stock into a 2-inch by 7-inch bookmark. Draw a symbol or symbols that show who you are. On the other side, write what each symbol means.

SYMBOLISM 14

Write a statement using *night* as a symbol for a larger, abstract idea.

_____

_____

_____

_____

_____

SYMBOLISM 15

Think of a symbol for *hope,* and use it in a sentence below.

_____

_____

_____

_____

_____

Hyperbole

HYPERBOLE 1

Hyperbole (high-PER-bol-ee) is figurative language that uses exaggeration.

I've told you _____ times to

pick up your clothes.

Check the choice that completes the sentence with hyperbole.

_____ two   _____ a hundred   _____ a million

HYPERBOLE 2

Draw lines to connect the hyperbole fragments to make a complete sentence.

1. If I've told you once,   even Einstein couldn't do them.

2. These math problems are so hard,   she even makes Cruella De Vil look good.

3 I want to win the game so bad,   I've told you a thousand times.

4. She's so mean,   I can taste it.

HYPERBOLE 3

Use hyperbole to complete the following:

The food was so overcooked _____

_____

_____

_____

_____

Hyperbole

HYPERBOLE 4

Hyperbole is often used in humor. Use hyperbole to complete the following:

The test was so hard that _____

_____

_____

_____

_____

HYPERBOLE 5

Use hyperbole to complete the following:

The town was so small _____

_____

_____

_____

_____

HYPERBOLE 6

Use hyperbole to complete the following:

The movie was so bad _____

_____

_____

_____

_____

HYPERBOLE 7

Use hyperbole to complete the following:

The car was so fast _____

_____

_____

_____

_____

Hyperbole

HYPERBOLE 8

Use hyperbole to complete the following:

The sky was so blue _____

_____

_____

The weather was so cold _____

_____

_____

HYPERBOLE 9

Use hyperbole to complete the following:

The gym shoes cost so much _____

_____

_____

_____

_____

HYPERBOLE 10

Use hyperbole to complete the following:

My dog is so smart

_____

_____

_____

_____

_____

HYPERBOLE 11

"The shot heard 'round the world" refers to the beginning of the American Revolutionary War. Why is this hyperbole?

_____

_____

_____

_____

Hyperbole

HYPERBOLE 12

"Time stood still." Why is this hyperbole?

_____

_____

_____

_____

_____

_____

HYPERBOLE 13

"I spent a month there one week" is hyperbole about a place. Check the word below that best describes the place:

_____ exciting

_____ busy

_____ dull

January						
Sunday	Monday	Tuesday	Wednesday	Thursday	Friday	Saturday
				1	2	3
4	5	6	7 Dr. App. 10 A.M.	8	9	10
11	12	13	14	15	16	17
18	19	20	21	22	23	24
25	26	27	28	29	30	31

HYPERBOLE 14

"His eyes shot daggers" is hyperbole describing someone's eyes. Check the phrase with the correct meaning.

_____ He had trick eyeglasses on.

_____ He was a spy.

_____ His eyes gave a violent look.

HYPERBOLE 15

"The woman's high voice could crack glass." This hyperbole means that the woman's voice was (check the best answer):

_____ strong.

_____ weak.

_____ untrained.

Hyperbole

HYPERBOLE 16

"That was the longest day of my life" is hyperbole about a day. Check the word below that best describes the day:

_____ fun

_____ sad

_____ boring

HYPERBOLE 17

Use hyperbole to complete the following:

The movie was so good

_____

_____

_____

_____

_____

HYPERBOLE 18

"You could fry an egg on the sidewalk" is hyperbole about the weather. Check the word below that best describes the temperature:

_____ balmy

_____ cold

_____ hot

HYPERBOLE 19

Use hyperbole to complete the following:

The sunset was so beautiful _____

_____

_____

_____

_____

_____

_____

Synecdoche

SYNECDOCHE 1

Synecdoche (suh-NEK-duh-kee) is figurative language in which a part is mentioned for the whole or a whole is mentioned for a part.

"Man, look at those cool wheels." Check the word that best shows the meaning of *wheels.*

_____ wheels   _____ tires   _____ car

SYNECDOCHE 2

"Where've you been, cowboy?" "I just herded 50 head into the high country."
Head refers to (check the best answer):

_____ cattle.

_____ brains.

_____ aces.

SYNECDOCHE 3

"The tap dancers pounded the boards."
In this sentence, *boards* means
(check the best answer):

_____ the stage.

_____ wooden planks.

_____ a hard test.

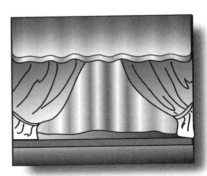

Synecdoche

SYNECDOCHE 4

"The crown imposed new taxes." Check the word or phrase that best shows the meaning of *crown.*

_____ head

_____ king or queen

_____ something worn on the head

SYNECDOCHE 5

"The hands will clean up when we're done." Check the word that best shows the meaning of *hands.*

_____ hands

_____ gloves

_____ workers

SYNECDOCHE 6

If someone said, "Look at those fancy threads!" what should you say in reply?

_____ "Quit insulting me."

_____ "Where?"

_____ "Thank you."

Threads means _____.

SYNECDOCHE 7

"I'm paying with plastic." What does *plastic* mean?

_____

_____

_____

_____

Synecdoche

SYNECDOCHE 8

"The Pentagon issued a statement today."

On your own paper, draw a cartoon that shows the literal meaning of this sentence (what the words say). Then draw another cartoon that shows the figurative meaning (what the intended meaning is).

SYNECDOCHE 9

"That pianist could really tickle the ivories!" Check the phrase that shows what the sentence means.

The pianist:

____ was good.

____ worked with elephants.

____ polished the piano keys.

SYNECDOCHE 10

"Jackson High won the basketball game." Check the choice to which *Jackson High* refers.

____ the coach

____ the team

____ the principal

SYNECDOCHE 11

"The law arrested the man for stealing." Check the choice to which *The law* refers.

____ the police officer

____ the lawyer

____ the judge

Synecdoche

SYNECDOCHE 12

The man looked at the Ferrari and said, "I guess that cost a pretty penny." In this sentence, what does *pretty penny* mean?

_____

_____

_____

_____

SYNECDOCHE 13

At dinner time, Grandma told Grandpa to come to the table for their daily bread. In this sentence, *bread* means (check the best answer):

_____ money.

_____ a loaf of bread.

_____ dinner.

SYNECDOCHE 14

On your own paper, draw two cartoons. One should illustrate the literal meaning of the sentence below (what the words say). One should illustrate the figurative meaning (what the intended meaning is).

The White House said the new policy will help U.S. citizens.

SYNECDOCHE 15

"Put Mozart on the stereo" really means

_____

_____

_____

_____

_____

Answer Keys

IMAGERY 1 (p. 2)
Answers will vary.

IMAGERY 2 (p. 2)
Underline: blue, pottery, yellow, black-flecked, large, red, pale, green.

IMAGERY 3–6 (p. 2–3)
Answers will vary.

IMAGERY 7 (p. 3)
1. scratchy ——— a. wool sweater
2. nubby b. angora fur
3. silky c. pillow
4. rough d. carpet
5. soft e. sandpaper

IMAGERY 8 (p. 4)
buzzed, dark, smell, scent, sizzling, mouth watered, stomach growled, crunchy, cold, hard, soft, red

IMAGERY 9–11 (p. 4–5)
Answers will vary.

IMAGERY 12 (p. 5)
basketball, cottonwood, Lake Erie, aloe vera, *Black Panther*, one-bedroom apartment

IMAGERY 13–14 (p. 5)
Answers will vary.

IMAGERY 15 (p. 6)
The first mug has a flower design. The second mug has a chip on the rim. The third mug has a checked design.

IMAGERY 16 (p. 6)
spicy, sweet, peppery, sour, bland, fruity

IMAGERY 17 (p. 6)
smooth, rough, hard, sharp, crusty

IMAGERY 18 (p. 7)
Answers will vary.

IMAGERY 19 (p. 7)
cry, splat, bark, thud, gurgle, tap, clomp, clap, swish

IMAGERY 20 (p. 7)
Answers will vary.

SIMILE 1 (p. 8)
2. Love is like a rose.
3. Love is as thorny as a rose.

SIMILE 2 (p. 8)
Answers will vary.

SIMILE 3 (p. 8)
Answers will vary, but should be something about March beginning with fierce weather and ending with mild weather.

SIMILE 4 (p. 8)
Answers will vary.

SIMILE 5 (p. 9)
A girl is being compared to a hyena.

SIMILE 6 (p. 9)
1. The opera star sang like a nightingale.
2. Seven people in the compact car were packed like sardines.
3. The preschool children were so wild, the room was like a three-ring circus.

SIMILE 7 (p. 9)
1. Sly as a fox
2. Quiet as a mouse
3. Gentle as a lamb
4. Wise as an owl

SIMILE 8 (p. 10)
a song.

SIMILE 9–10 (p. 10)
Answers will vary.

SIMILE 11 (p. 10)
My dog smells like gym socks.

SIMILE 12–17 (p. 11–12)
Answers will vary.

SIMILE 18 (p. 12)
A rainbow is like a box of crayons.

METAPHOR 1 (p. 13)
Love is a rose.

METAPHOR 2 (p. 13)
My grandfather is slow.

METAPHOR 3–4 (p. 13–14)
Answers will vary.

METAPHOR 5 (p. 14)
Homework is being compared to an avalanche. It means that I have too much homework to be able to go to the movie.

METAPHOR 6 (p. 14)
Answers will vary.

METAPHOR 7 (p. 14)
Your thinking is compared to a train that has gone off the track. The question means your thinking has a problem.

METAPHOR 8 (p. 15)
Answers will vary.

METAPHOR 9 (p. 15)
No. Ann is special because it's her birthday.

METAPHOR 10–11 (p. 15–16)
Answers will vary.

METAPHOR 12 (p. 16)
Steven is being compared to a snake. Paths will vary.

METAPHOR 13 (p. 16)
Answers will vary, but may mention that the metaphor is more direct and, therefore, more powerful.

METAPHOR 14 (p. 16)
My classroom is hot.

METAPHOR 15–18 (p. 17–18)
Answers will vary.

METAPHOR 19 (p. 18)
The teacher would not bend or break the rules.

METAPHOR 20 (p. 18)
Answers will vary.

ADAGE 1 (p. 19)
Answers will vary, but should say something about leaving things alone, not stirring up trouble.

ADAGE 2 (p. 19)
Answers will vary.

ADAGE 3 (p. 19)
rings

ADAGE 4 (p. 19)
Answers will vary.

ADAGE 5 (p. 20)
Be good to those who provide for you.

ADAGE 6 (p. 20)
No pain, no gain.

ADAGE 7 (p. 20)
Answers will vary, but should say something about what you think you can do affects how successful you are.

ADAGE 8–9 (p. 21)
Answers will vary.

ADAGE 10 (p. 21)
1. Answers will vary, but should say something about the importance of taking care of small problems before they get bigger.
2. Answers will vary.

ADAGE 11 (p. 21)
1. Answers will vary. The best answer will mention a metal.
2. Answers will vary.

ADAGE 12–13 (p. 22)
Answers will vary.

ADAGE 14 (p. 22)
play.

ADAGE 15 (p. 22)
A picture is worth a thousand words.

ADAGE 16–17 (p. 23)
Answers will vary.

ADAGE 18 (p. 23)
People always think someone else is better off than they are.

IDIOM 1 (p. 24)
What's the news?

IDIOM 2 (p. 24)
One picture should show cats and dogs falling from the sky, the other should show a rain downpour.

IDIOM 3 (p. 24)
I'm going to bed.

IDIOM 4 (p. 25)
Tanya was so nervous that her stomach felt fluttery.

IDIOM 5 (p. 25)
burn the midnight oil

IDIOM 6 (p. 25)
Mum's the word.

IDIOM 7 (p. 25)
blow your own horn

IDIOM 8 (p. 26)
Answers will vary, but *all thumbs* should mean "clumsy," *bite the bullet* should mean "be determined," and *an albatross around my neck* should mean "a burden."

IDIOM 9 (p. 26)
has his dander up, got up on the wrong side of the bed, has a bee in her bonnet

IDIOM 10 (p. 26)
Answers will vary, but the meaning of the phrase is "I'm going to do everything I can to annoy you."

IDIOM 11 (p. 27)
I'll pull strings and cut the red tape for you.

IDIOM 12 (p. 27)
by the rules.

IDIOM 13 (p. 27)
she had to handle a messy situation.

IDIOM 14 (p. 27)
Answers will vary, but the meaning should be that critics feared the singer would not be able to continue making hit recordings.

IDIOM 15 (p. 28)
No. Answers will vary, but "elbow grease" means scrubbing by hand or hard physical labor.

IDIOM 16 (p. 28)
he was taking a nap.

IDIOM 17 (p. 28)
1. Answers will vary, but should show "once in a blue moon" to mean "rarely," "put on the dog" to mean "to dress up extremely" or "to make fancy," and "pay the piper" to mean "to pay for service rendered."
2. Answers will vary.

IDIOM 18 (p. 28)
1. are the boss.
2. ask what's wrong.

CLICHÉ 1 (p. 29)
1. mule
2. lamb
3. waste
4. heels
5. fiddle

CLICHÉ 2–3 (p. 29)
Answers will vary.

CLICHÉ 4 (p. 29)
Answers will vary, but should mean that one is out of place in one's surroundings.

CLICHÉ 5 (p. 30)
Yes, it means the friend slept well.

CLICHÉ 6 (p. 30)
Answers will vary.

CLICHÉ 7 (p. 30)
hard as a diamond

CLICHÉ 8 (p. 30)
goose.

CLICHÉ 9–15 (p. 31–33)
Answers will vary.

CLICHÉ 16 (p. 33)
The speed of light is 299,792,458 meters per second, or 186,282 miles per second (<www.ask.com.>) According to the book *It's Raining Frogs and Fishes* by Jerry Dennis, lightning bolts travel at speeds up to 93,000 miles per second.

CLICHÉ 17–18 (p. 33–34)
Answers will vary.

CLICHÉ 19 (p. 34)
Answers will vary, but could include embarrassment, anger, and sunburn.

CLICHÉ 20 (p. 34)
No. Answers will vary, but could be something like "I was terrified."

PERSONIFICATION 1 (p. 35)
smiled

PERSONIFICATION 2 (p. 35)
cruel

PERSONIFICATION 3 (p. 35)
1. winked
2. looked, smile

PERSONIFICATION 4 (p. 35)
1. danced
2. babbled, soothing lullaby, ambled

PERSONIFICATION 5 (p. 36)
The ocean waved goodbye.

PERSONIFICATION 6–12 (p. 36–37)
Answers will vary.

PERSONIFICATION 13 (p. 38)
coughed, sputtered

PERSONIFICATION 14 (p. 38)
Answers will vary.

PERSONIFICATION 15 (p. 38)
The cactus brings us blooms in the spring.

PERSONIFICATION 16 (p. 39)
Answers will vary.

PERSONIFICATION 17 (p. 39)
Jaycee caught the bus to go downtown to the library. As she gripped her seat tightly, the bus <u>darted</u> through traffic <u>like a soccer player avoiding defenders</u>. When it finally <u>deposited</u> her at the library, Jaycee heaved a sigh of relief. She stepped inside and felt the <u>warm welcome the library always offered her</u>. The <u>comforting sights and smells of the familiar books</u> were <u>like old friends greeting her</u>. She couldn't wait to find a new adventure in one of the <u>books displayed like soldiers waiting to be shipped out on a new mission</u>.

ALLUSION 1 (p. 40)
Winnie-the-Pooh. Answers will vary, but should indicate that Michael is a pessimist; he always thinks the worst will happen.

ALLUSION 2 (p. 40)
Someone from a lowly background becomes highly successful.

ALLUSION 3 (p. 40)
"Have you been where you were not supposed to go?"

ALLUSION 4 (p. 41)
The Wizard of Oz

ALLUSION 5 (p. 41)
Answers will vary, but should indicate that she entered without permission.

ALLUSION 6 (p. 41)
She is a detective.

ALLUSION 7 (p. 41)
He acts like a boy.

ALLUSION 8 (p. 42)
long.

ALLUSION 9 (p. 42)
Answers will vary, but should indicate that Dr. Seuss' The Cat in the Hat made a big mess, left, and got the children into trouble.

ALLUSION 10 (p. 42)
Answers will vary, but should indicate that the person needs a heart.

ALLUSION 11 (p. 42)
Smokey Bear, whose motto is "Only you can prevent forest fires."

ALLUSION 12 (p. 43)
he gets into everything.

ALLUSION 13 (p. 43)
the Ugly Duckling.

ALLUSION 14 (p. 43)
Answers will vary.

ALLUSION 15 (p. 43)
"The Three Little Pigs."

SYMBOLISM 1 (p. 44)
Answers will vary.

SYMBOLISM 2 (p. 44)
a diploma

SYMBOLISM 3–4 (p. 44–45)
Answers will vary.

SYMBOLISM 5 (p. 45)
old age

SYMBOLISM 6 (p. 45)
owl

SYMBOLISM 7 (p. 45)
dove

SYMBOLISM 8 (p. 46)
hawk

SYMBOLISM 9 (p. 46)
green

SYMBOLISM 10 (p. 46)
sadness.

SYMBOLISM 11 (p. 46)
a road

SYMBOLISM 12 (p. 47)
eternity

SYMBOLISM 13–15 (p. 47)
Answers will vary.

HYPERBOLE 1 (p. 48)
a million

HYPERBOLE 2 (p. 48)
1. If I've told you once, I've told you a thousand times.
2. These math problems are so hard, even Einstein couldn't do them.
3 I want to win the game so bad, I can taste it.
4. She's so mean, she even makes Cruella De Vil look good.

HYPERBOLE 3–10 (p. 48–50)
Answers will vary.

HYPERBOLE 11 (p. 50)
Answers will vary, but should indicate that a gunshot could really be heard for only a short distance.

HYPERBOLE 12 (p. 51)
Answers will vary, but should indicate that time cannot stand still.

HYPERBOLE 13 (p. 51)
dull

HYPERBOLE 14 (p. 51)
His eyes gave a violent look.

HYPERBOLE 15 (p. 51)
strong.

HYPERBOLE 16 (p. 52)
boring

HYPERBOLE 17 (p. 52)
Answers will vary.

HYPERBOLE 18 (p. 52)
hot

HYPERBOLE 19 (p. 52)
Answers will vary.

SYNECDOCHE 1 (p. 53)
car

SYNECDOCHE 2 (p. 53)
cattle.

SYNECDOCHE 3 (p. 53)
the stage.

SYNECDOCHE 4 (p. 54)
king or queen

SYNECDOCHE 5 (p. 54)
workers

SYNECDOCHE 6 (p. 54)
"Thank you." *Threads* means "clothing."

SYNECDOCHE 7 (p. 54)
credit or debit card, but usually credit card

SYNECDOCHE 8 (p. 55)
Answers will vary, but one picture should show a talking pentagonal building, and the other should show a military man or the secretary of defense speaking.

SYNECDOCHE 9 (p. 55)
was good.

SYNECDOCHE 10 (p. 55)
the team

SYNECDOCHE 11 (p. 55)
the police officer

SYNECDOCHE 12 (p. 56)
Answers will vary, but should indicate a lot of money.

SYNECDOCHE 13 (p. 56)
dinner.

SYNECDOCHE 14 (p. 56)
Answers will vary, but one picture should show a talking White House, and another should show the president or the president's representative speaking.

SYNECDOCHE 15 (p. 56)
Answers will vary, but should mean playing a Mozart CD on the stereo.